Master Your Life By Mastering Your Message

Make An Incredible Impact On Your Business & Life By Applying 15 Steps To Improve Your Image Through Your Written Words!

When communication fails, the costs are countless. Business deals are lost. Relationships are ruined. Hearts are broken.

In this amazing Itty Bitty Book, Sarah Coolidge shows you how becoming the Master of your written words will increase your success in all areas and support you to create a thriving business and a joyful life.

Master the steps in this book and you will be able to use all of today's written technology, including websites, emails, and self-publishing to win customers, clients and friends.

For example:

- Create a compelling and convincing first impression.
- Build rapport and connection with your reader.
- Set yourself apart as the best in your field.

Your Amazing Itty Bitty® Message Mastery Book

15 Simple Steps to Improving Your Image through Your Written Words

Sarah Coolidge, MA

Published by Itty Bitty® Publishing
A subsidiary of S & P Productions, Inc.

Printed in the United States of America

Itty Bitty® Publishing
311 Main Street, Suite D
El Segundo, CA 90245
(310) 640-8885

ISBN: 978-1-931191-09-8

Dedicated to my mom, who was relentless in correcting my English;

My dad, who knew better than most, the challenges of communicating when language fails us;

And to my children, who are the future for us all.

Stop by our Itty Bitty® website to find interesting blog entries regarding **Mastering Your Written Communication.**

www.IttyBittyPublishing.com

You can reach Sarah Coolidge by sending an email to Sarah @typozappers.com or calling 530-426-Typo (8976)

Table of Contents

Introduction

In this Itty Bitty Book you will find ideas and methods for honing your written communication so that you maximize the likelihood that your target audience is going to receive the message you are trying to send.

Why does this matter to you? Because, as a businessperson, you know the importance of your image in the client's mind.

One of the ways a prospect will decide if they want to do business with you is by how you present yourself in your written word. Like it or not, when they read your material, they are going to make judgments about you. They will assess your professionalism and your ability to perform the work you promise based on your writing.

If your message is confusing or filled with errors, they will not buy.

You must take control of the message you send. This book will give you the tools and information you need to become the Master of Your Message.

Enjoy!

Sarah Coolidge
June 17, 2016

Step 1
The Power of Words

In this Itty Bitty Book you will find 15 simple
things you can do to enhance your written
messages and reduce the chance of damaging
your image and losing business through errors in
your writing.

1. When the proper words are used in the proper
   way, communication is enhanced.
2. Right or wrong, people often judge each
   other by the words they use or misuse.
3. Communication is diminished when you have
   a limited vocabulary.
4. Ineffective communication leads to
   confusion.
5. A confused mind does not buy, or even stay
   interested.

Enhancing the effectiveness of your communication enhances all of your relationships.

TIPS: Why Language is Incredible

Words allow you to:

- Share experiences with one another. Talk, whisper, scream and sing your messages.
- Connect even when separated by distance. Writing letters, phone messaging and emails all use words to reach across distances that would otherwise prevent you from communicating.
- Close a gap in time. Written words allow you to share your experience with future generations, expanding your influence far beyond your own lifetime.

You, like most of us, acquired language easily and naturally as a young child and use it throughout your life without ever realizing the amazing impact it carries for you.

Step 2
Become the Master of Your Message

When you take responsibility for every part of the communication process that is under your control, you will reap a multitude of rewards:

1. Happier relationships with friends and family.
2. An easier job of parenting.
3. Smoother interactions out in the world.
4. A sweeter love life.
5. Increased sales and customers who love you.
6. A fabulous image as a professional with high integrity.
7. Increased peace of mind and confidence, because you know you are doing your best.
8. You are more likely to have your needs met which leads to a happier life in general.

This is why you want to become the Master of your Message.

TIPS: Why Do Words Sometimes Fail You?

- You might be using vocabulary the receiver does not understand.
- Your body language or tone of voice might be sending out a conflicting message, confusing your partner.
- Your vocabulary is not adequate to the task.
- When speaking, your listener is distracted by your mispronunciations, misused words or accent.
- When writing, your reader is distracted by your grammar, spelling or punctuation mistakes.
- Any number of other distractions can be confusing the interaction.

Effective communication depends on a huge variety of factors, and anything you can do to limit the impact of these other influences is going to enhance the likelihood of your message being understood.

Step 3
Living Language

Human beings are set apart from all of the other living creatures on this planet by one incredible development: language.

1. Without words, you depend on body language to communicate.
2. Experts estimate that non-verbal messages accounts for over 93% of our communication.
3. There are over 6,000 languages in the world today.
4. A baby's spoken vocabulary will grow from zero to 5,000 words in the first five years of life.
5. An average person uses about 20,000 words regularly and has another 20,000 on reserve.
6. An estimated 1,000 words are added to English language dictionaries every year.

Human language is alive, growing and changing all of the time, just as you are.

TIPS: Writing That Living Language

Remember:

- Your words are only about 7% of your message.
- When someone can see you, either live or on video, they will be able to use your non-verbal communication to help them understand your message.
- Your writing does not have any of the information that your body language and tonality usually provides.
- You want to maximize the chance that your reader will understand.
- When you write, your vocabulary had better be precise.
- There is no room for ambiguity.

Step 4
The Magic of Writing

What is so important about writing? For one thing, before we had ways to record your thoughts, all the information you held in your head would disappear when you died.

1. Most information was lost to history until the written word unlocked people's ability to create messages for anyone, anytime.
2. People are wired for telling and listening to stories since that was our first way to pass information from one generation to the next.
3. Writing allows you to overcome distance and time with your communication.
4. Written words are dependent on others having the ability to read in order to communicate.
5. There are rules in writing (grammar, punctuation and spelling) to reduce confusion and clarify your message as much as possible.
6. Effective writing can communicate clearly and powerfully, even though it is arguably our weakest communication method.

TIPS: Improve Your Communication

- Think about your message before you start to relay it. What are the crucial points?
- Think about your audience. What experiences have they had that might color their interpretation of your message? Can you do anything to offset potential problems?
- Get simple and clear. Pretend that your audience will have to remember everything you are sending out. Any extra detail or unclear meanings may prevent your message from being understood and retained.
- Everyone has preferred communication styles. Try to send your message in more than one way so all of your audience can receive it.

Remember, we have rules about language to make it easier to communicate clearly, not to make your life difficult!

Step 5
Enhancing Your Life and Your Business in Today's Writing World

Like it or not, prospective employers, customers and friends all expect to be able find out more about you online. You must take control of what they find.

1. Google your name and your business name and see what shows up.
2. Search online directories in your area for information about you and your business.
3. For every reference to you that you find, make sure that the information is correct and up-to-date.
4. You won't be able to remove negative reviews from the review sites, but you can often bury them with positive ones.
5. Interact with anyone you can as you do this online investigation. If someone has written about you in any way, thank them.
6. Take steps to make sure that your website, social media accounts and blogs are current.
7. Respond quickly when people accept your invitation to interact with you online.

If all this seems like too much, consider hiring a virtual assistant to take it on.

TIPS: Online Business Writing

Published writers have clout, online or on paper.
How can you use that to your advantage?

- Start a blog about your area of expertise and post to it regularly. Spend some time studying how to attract visitors to build your audience.
- Write a newsletter to send out to your email list. Keeping people informed and connected will help them to remember you when it is time for them to buy.
- Write an expert report on your specialty and post it on LinkedIn and other social media.
- Investigate the self-publishing world to decide if writing a business card book is right for you. It can be very impressive to hand people your book in place of a card and is often a great marketing investment.
- Make sure your website is current with compelling and interesting content.
- Study the email world, and how to write a great subject line which is more likely to get your email opened. Then, make sure the content of the email is interesting and error-free.

Step 6
First Impressions

You know the statistics: new acquaintances will sum you up in their minds and make a decision about you within one-tenth of a second of first meeting you.

1. First impressions are based on a lot of visual information and once made, can be impossible to unmake.
2. A first impression can have a huge impact on the success of your business, and life in general.
3. People you meet will be deciding if they think you are:
    a. Likeable
    b. Trustworthy
    c. Interesting
    d. Worth Knowing
4. The cosmetics, fashion, perfume, and image consulting industries are all built around the power of the first impression.
5. When you speak, your first impression is solidified or undermined by your:
    a. Accent
    b. Enunciation
    c. Tone of voice
    d. Vocabulary

TIPS: Creating a Great First Impression When You Write

Every unsolicited email, web page, Facebook post, or book that you write is an opportunity to make a fabulous first impression on someone.

- Let your passion for the work you do show by being interesting and informative.
- Your attention to detail will be evident by the lack of errors.
- Put your reader at ease by making sure your sentences flow in a logical, clear manner.
- Demonstrate your professionalism by presenting the highest quality in spelling, punctuation and grammar.
- Show your high regard for your reader by making sure your tone is respectful, appropriate and clear.
- Value them and your relationship with them by doing everything you can to communicate clearly.

Whether it is an entry in a dating site profile or your resume, do everything possible to make sure you shine!

Step 7
Grammar

Grammar is the fancy word for the rules of speech and writing, and you use it every day, even if you don't think you know it at all.

1. Grammar rules developed because people needed agreements on how to communicate more effectively.
2. Grammar standardizes the way we speak and write so that we can concentrate on our message.
3. Writing is arguably most people's weakest form of communication.
4. Learning about English grammar will make you a more effective writer.
5. Learning about grammar in general will give you a basis for learning and understanding a second language.
6. Grammar gives you the language to talk about your language.
7. Descriptive grammarians are interested in the rules you use to communicate in the living world. They are also known as linguists.
8. Prescriptive grammarians study the rules that describe the correct or incorrect use of the language. They are often teachers or editors.

TIPS: Gussy Up Your Grammar

- Make sure your pronouns and objects match.
  *e.g. The **girls** changed **their** dresses.*
    Not- *The **girls** changed **her** dresses.*
- Write complete sentences that have at least a subject and a verb.
  e.g. Dogs bark.
- Don't confuse objects with people.
  *e.g. He is an astronaut **who** likes to fly. There is the spaceship **that** he likes the most.*
- *Than* is for comparisons, *then* is for time.
  *e.g. When you have lived longer **than** me, **then** you will understand.*
- Be sure that your subject and verb are in agreement:
  *e.g. The **people were** angry. (A plural subject.) The **person was** angry. (A singular subject.)*

These are just a few examples of some common grammatical errors.

In general, if you take a moment to read what you have written aloud, you will often hear when something is off and be able to fix it, even if grammar is not your strong suit.

Step 8
Spelling

By now I hope you are convinced that taking the time to make your written work as presentable as possible is worthwhile. Proper spelling is just another part of that.

1. There are lots of rules that can assist you. Remember "when two vowels go walking, the first one does the talking?"
2. Break words into syllables and learn to recognize commonalities. Gumption, traction and function all have –tion to help you group them in your mind.
3. Learn the meanings of the word parts. For example, the prefix con- in connect, convene and congregate, always means "with."
4. Use your spell check system to study and learn from your errors.
5. Read! The more you read, the more words just begin to look right or wrong to you when you write them.
6. Learn the proper pronunciation of a word. You will be more likely to spell it properly when you sound it out.

TIPS: Study Up On Spelling

These are some commonly misspelled and misused words. Do you know them all?

- Principal/principle
- Its/it's
- There/they're/their
- Personal/personnel
- Capital/capitol
- To/two/too
- Prey/pray
- Accept/except
- Compliment/complement
- Ensure/insure/assure
- Dessert/dessert
- Morale/moral
- Lay/lie
- Peek/pique/peak
- Weather/wether/whether
- Gorilla/guerilla

If you have problem words that you know give you trouble, make it a habit to double-check them with an online dictionary every time you write.

Step 9
Punctuation

Spend a few minutes listening to people talk around you and you will notice that they pause every so often to take a breath, emphasize a point or switch topics. That is what punctuation does for you when you read and write.

1. The first written texts just had all the wordsrunningtogetherlikethisandnopunctuati oncanyouimaginehowconfusingthatwas
2. Although there were some earlier attempts, punctuation did not really take hold until the 8th century.
3. Spaces between words make it easier to read and periods at the ends of sentences allow your eyes to rest for a bit of time.
4. Commas, dashes, brackets, parentheses, colons and semicolons all serve to help you pause or clarify your topic.
5. Exclamation points and question marks help you to mimic speech and add interest.
6. Punctuation stopped evolving when the printing press was developed, but is beginning to change again with the advent of texting, emoticons and computers in general.

TIPS: Primp Up Your Punctuation

- The most common use of a colon (:) is to introduce a list.
  e.g. The flag had three colors: red, white and blue.

- The semicolon (;) is used when that list has some commas in it.
  e.g. The flag had three colors: bright, scarlet red; brilliant, snowy white; and intense, sky blue.

- Commas tell you when to pause and are used to separate items in a list, among many other things. Be careful not to overuse them!

- Quotation marks are for direct copies of someone's speech or text, <u>not</u> for *setting something apart as special.* Use italics, bolding or underlining for that.

- Dashes and hyphens are different. Hyphens are for connecting two words to form a super-word (also called a hyphenated compound word). Dashes emphasize a part – a really important part – of your sentence.

- Exclamation points demonstrate excitement. One is enough!

- When there is a question, use a question mark. Warning: this does not mean that every sentence with a question word (who, what, where, when or how) will end with a question mark.

Step 10
Vocabulary: Why Care?

English is a particularly rich language, and by some estimates, has over one million words.

So what's the big deal about vocabulary?

1. A good vocabulary increases your precision in communication, enabling you to communicate more clearly.
2. The more words you know, the more options you have. If one attempt fails, you can regroup and try another.
3. A small vocabulary increases the level of frustration in communication. The participants are more likely to give up and communication fails.
4. Many researchers consider someone's vocabulary level as the best single predictor of their future accomplishments.
5. Children with vocabulary deficiencies are more likely to fail in school, which can impact their success in life.

TIPS: Ideas for Building Your Vocabulary

- Make the dictionary your friend. Look up every word you wonder about, either online or in an old-fashioned book.
- Get a Word-a-Day Calendar and use it. In a year you will expand your vocabulary by 365 words.
- Or, you can get on a Word-a-Day email list.
- Install a vocabulary building app on your phone.
- Make it a game. Pick unfamiliar words out of your daily conversations and look them up. Then use them the next day.
- Play word games like crossword puzzles, word searches and charades.
- A majority of English words have Greek and Latin roots. When you learn those roots, you will be able to use them to decipher meanings of many unknown words.
- READ! Reading is the best (and most fun) way to grow your vocabulary. Supercharge this method by taking the time to look up unfamiliar words.

Expand your creativity and communication by expanding your vocabulary.

Step 11
Today's Tools of the Trade

These days there are all sorts of tools and services designed to speed up and simplify your writing life.

1. Online dictionaries and thesauruses.
2. The word-processing program on your computer.
3. There are many websites and blogs devoted to helping you find just the right word, sentence structure and punctuation.
4. The spelling and grammar checking functions of your word processing program can teach you a lot.
5. The autocorrect functions on your computer and smartphone can also expand your written world.
6. Voice recognition systems will transcribe your spoken words if you don't want to type or handwrite.
7. Transcriptionists and online freelance services can write, edit and proofread for you.

All of these can make your job as a writer much easier and are a wonderful boon to those who don't enjoy writing at all.

TIPS: Why You Must be Careful with These Tools

Just like many things in life, there are downsides to using these tools. Remember:

- Double-check your spell check! A word may be spelled correctly, but it can still be the wrong word for your meaning.
- Look at more than one source before you make a decision on spelling a funky word, hiring a specialist, or buying any software.
- Double-check when you study words online because English is different throughout the world. What is proper in England may sound strange in the United States, and vice-versa.
- Garbage in, garbage out. Any system you use is still dependent on what you put into it.
- You get what you pay for. Because all of these methods can be very low-cost, or free, don't be surprised if you receive low-quality.
- You must review what you get back. Your name and reputation are at stake, and you alone are responsible for the message you are putting out.

Use these tools as you need them, but don't forget that they are just tools. *You* are the Master!

Step 12
Make It As Easy As Possible
For Your Reader

Once you have mastered your message, it is time
to do everything you can to make sure the
message is received.

1. Define the goal of your writing. The most
    common reasons to write are to entertain,
    persuade, inform or teach the reader.
2. Research the likely reading level of your
    audience. As an example, if you are running
    for office, you want to write your campaign
    material for the reading level of the average
    voter in your district.
3. Study and emulate the works of other authors
    who you enjoy, and who are effectively
    reaching their audiences.
4. Whatever you write, you must take some
    time to think about the reader before you
    start. Most likely they are busy and want to
    know quickly if reading your material is
    going to be worth their time. It is your job to
    convince them that it is.

TIPS: Connect To Your Audience

While you cannot force others to understand you, there are many steps you can take to make it easier for them to stay connected and increase the likelihood that they will read your whole message.

- Know your audience. The average reader in the United States reads at the 9th grade level but prefers material written at the 7th grade level.
- Use an active voice in your writing, with the subjects of your sentences performing the action.
- Vary your sentence and paragraph length. This prevents monotony.
- Use those big, obscure words only when they are necessary for precision and accuracy.
- Don't use jargon, unless it is used by your audience. The same goes for technical terms and acronyms.
- Practice ways to surprise your readers and to stimulate their curiosity. Then they will want to keep reading, which is why mystery novels can be so successful.

Make it your goal to be informative, fun and welcoming to your readers.

Step 13
Keeping It Simple

You are reading an Itty Bitty Book.

1. Have you noticed how it is written?
2. In today's world, everything is accelerated. People are scanning through information, looking for clues to tell them if they want to read more or move on to something else.
3. Very few people have the time, or the energy, to read a full-length book. Yet, they still crave knowledge.

Itty Bitty Books are answering that need in a very deliberate way. We do this by:

1. Chunking information into smaller ideas.
2. Using headlines and highlighted text.
3. Using lots of white space.
4. Using lots of bulleted lists.
5. Using an active voice.
6. Keeping the book short.

Itty Bitty authors use all of these techniques because it's easier for you, the reader, to satisfy your need for information.

TIPS: More Ideas for Keeping it Simple

- Study writers that you like. There are tons of blogs written for writers. Find some favorites and copy their style (NOT their material!).
- Find a seventh grader and ask them to read your material. Then ask them to tell you if they understand it and if they have suggestions for improvement.
- Read your writing aloud. Do you stumble on the words? Does it sound to you like a conversational, relaxed tone? Refine it until it does.
- Re-read it again and look for any extra words you can eliminate and any opportunities to create a bulleted list.

Writers tend to write at a level that is comfortable for them. That does not mean that their readers will understand what they have written!
Simpler is usually better.

Step 14
Ghostwriters, Editors, Proofreaders

Ghostwriters, editors and proofreaders are the Three Musketeers of the writing world. They support you as the Master of Your Message.

1. If you have a powerful message to share with the world but no inclination, time or ability to write it out, hire a ghostwriter.
   a. Ghostwriters write it for you.
   b. You get to call yourself the author.
2. Regardless of who wrote your material, you will benefit from the expertise of an editor.
   a. Editors assist you with the flow of your content.
   b. Editors also make recommendations for material to add or remove.
3. When you THINK your material is ready to send out to the world, it is time to call in the proofreader.
   a. Proofreaders read through your copy one last time with fresh eyes, correcting errors in punctuation, spelling and grammar.
   b. Proofreaders also adjust errors in pagination, references and formatting.

TIPS: Doing it All Yourself

Occasionally you will not have the time or resources to hire professionals to assist you with your work. What can you do?

- Run your material through your spell-check program and really look at the underlined words. It seems crazy, but a lot of people don't even bother to do this one simple step.
- You can also run it through a grammar checking program to look for errors.
- Re-read it at least five or six times.
- Set what you wrote aside for a chunk of time, overnight if possible. Then read it again with your rested eyes.
- Your brain knows what you wanted to say as you were writing so it often fills in missing words that are not actually on the page when you re-read your material, making you believe that the words are there. You can get around this by reading your work aloud or reading it backwards (yes, backwards!).

All writers are subject to developing blind spots towards their own work, as well as becoming attached to it and overly sensitive to other's input. That's why editing and proofing your own work is risky business and should be avoided if possible.

Step 15
When to Call In a Pro

Many people think that they don't need a professional ghostwriter, editor or proofreader unless they write a book.

1. This can be a big mistake for your business, especially if your business depends on that critical first impression people get from reading your:
   a. Blog posts
   b. LinkedIn articles
   c. Marketing materials
   d. Emails
   e. EBooks
   f. Websites
2. If you are producing such content regularly, you should have someone checking it.
3. The goal is to cast the best light on you and your business by producing the clearest writing possible.
4. If people read your materials and are confused, they won't do business with you.
5. If they find a multitude of mistakes in what you write, they will conclude that you don't care about quality and again, they won't buy from you. You can't afford that, can you?

TIPS: Where to Find Help

Now that you are convinced that you should have another pair of eyes reviewing your work, where will you find them?

- If you have limited time and budget, you can ask co-workers, friends and family. When doing so, try to pick people who have the highest likelihood of being helpful to you.
- When you have more time but still a limited budget, you can use options like Craigslist, online freelancers and college interns.
- As your budget allows, and the impact of your writing becomes more critical to your success, you will want to turn to experienced professionals.

For all of these, choose carefully and evaluate their qualifications, experience and motives. You want someone who cares enough to be honest with you and who will do a good job for you.

For a FREE consultation on polishing your writing, please send an email to the author: sarah@typozappers.com.

Congratulations!

You've finished. Before you go…

Tweet/share that you finished this book.

Please star rate this book.

Reviews are solid gold to writers. Please take a few minutes to give us some itty bitty feedback.

ABOUT THE AUTHOR

Sarah Coolidge grew up in a household which was uniquely focused on communication and the English language. Her mother was a second-generation English major, who constantly reminded Sarah and her sisters to "aspirate your h's" and "enunciate!" Her father suffered from speech aphasia as the result of a cerebral aneurysm, and had difficulty constructing complete, understandable sentences. This complex environment brought an intense focus to the impact of language to her childhood and life.

Sarah specializes in supporting entrepreneurs, small business people and website builders to present their best possible written messages to the world. She is a sought-after proofreader in the self-publishing industry and the co-author of "Make a Book, Move a Book, Book a Sale." "Your Amazing Itty Bitty® Message Mastery Book" is her second book.

Ms. Coolidge resides in Tahoe Vista, California, and can be reached by emailing:

sarah@typozappers.com.

**If you enjoyed this Itty Bitty® book,
you might also enjoy…**

- **Your Amazing Itty Bitty® Travel Planning Book** – Rosemary Workman

- **Your Amazing Itty Bitty® Cancer Book** – Jacqueline Kreple

- **Your Amazing Itty Bitty® Self-Esteem Book** – Jade Elizabeth

And many other Itty Bitty® Books
available online.